Speech Companion

A Carefree Coloring Book for Adults

Dominique Kennedy

About the Author

Dominique Kennedy is an experienced and certified Speech-Language Pathologist. Dominique earned a bachelor's degree and master's degree in Communication Sciences and Disorders with an emphasis in Speech-Language Pathology. Her experience across settings includes schools, hospitals, rehabilitation centers, and early intervention. Through her private practice, she serves children and adults. She is a member of the American Speech-Language-Hearing Association (ASHA) and Special Interest Groups (SIGs) Fluency & Fluency Disorders and Augmentative & Alternative Communication. Through her desire to empower families, she has developed educational programs, professional development courses, and workshops. Dominique lives in the Atlanta Metro area of Georgia with her husband and their two daughters. She enjoys fine arts, music, and culture.

Speech Companion

A Carefree Coloring Book for Adults

Contents

Author's Note

This idea of developing the *"Speech Companion"* was sparked shortly after the publication of my first book entitled, *"Stuttering, It's What You Think."* As a speech and hearing professional, I frequently have others approach me to determine how they can improve their speech, either for personal reasons or for professional reasons. Often, parents will contact me to provide intervention services to improve their child's overall communication skills. One of the most frequently asked questions that I get from parents and caregivers is, "What can I do at home to help my loved one with their speech?" The concept of book pairs or book companions was born as a solution to this voiced concern.

The caregiver-as-coach approach is encouraged when purchasing your *"Speech Companion"* and *"Speech Culture"* book pair. *"Speech Companion: A Carefree Coloring Book for Adults"* is a resource that may be paired with *"Speech Culture: A Companion Coloring Book of Short-Stories for Kids."* The essence of each character's name in "Speech Culture" directly corresponds to the terms used in "Speech Companion." Pay close attention to each character's name and name meaning in your child's book as its meaning is expanded into an "I Am" statement within each publication. The "Speech Culture" coloring book contains powerful, practical tools for kids to elevate their speech and language skills.

As a Speech-Language Pathologist, I take pride in partnering with individuals and families in getting the most out of communicative opportunities, whether it be self-directed or within an exchange. One of my statements of philosophy reads as follows: *...foster an environment that reinforces the positive impact that words have on the human spirit---one family at a time..".* I desire that this publication serves as a resource to reinforce mindfulness and positive thinking by promoting self-comments or words that are affirming. On a simple level, if you so choose, I hope that your "Speech Companion" be enjoyed in a carefree, relaxing way.

If you enjoyed your "Speech Companion," please feel free to contact me and consider telling a friend.

Best,

Dominique Kennedy, MS, CCC-SLP

I AM RIGHTEOUS

1 I AM RIGHTEOUS

I AM
ROBUST

I AM PROLIFIC

I AM

INNOVATIVE

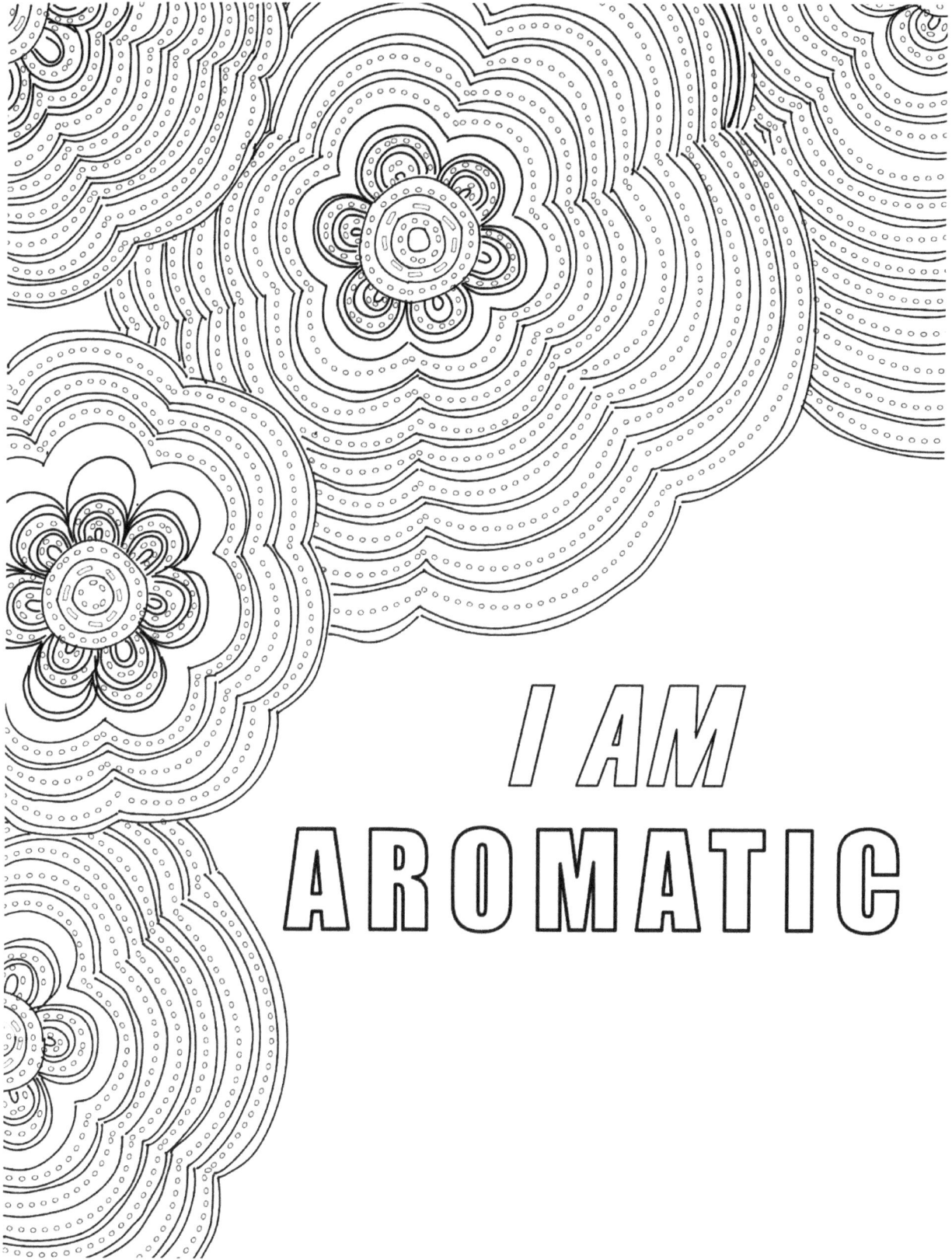

I AM
AROMATIC

I AM
MAGNANIMOUS

I AM
MUNIFICENT

I AM
GLORIOUS

I AM

9 I AM

I AM

I AM

I AM

12 I AM

I AM

I AM

13 I AM

I AM

I AM

15 I AM

Glossary:

Aromatic- having a noticeable and pleasant smell; having a distinctive quality

Glorious- possessing or deserving glory: illustrious; marked by great beauty or splendor: magnificent

Innovative- characterized by, tending to, or introducing innovations

Magnanimous- showing or suggesting a lofty and courageous spirit; showing or suggesting nobility of feeling and generosity of mind

Munificent- characterized by great liberality or generosity

Prolific- marked by abundant inventiveness or productivity

Righteous- morally right or justifiable; genuine, excellent

Robust- having or exhibiting strength or vigorous health; strongly formed or constructed: sturdy

Reference

Webster, M. 2020. Retrieved July 7, 2020, from https://www.merriam-webster.com/dictionary/

www.ingramcontent.com/pod-product-compliance
Lightning Source LLC
Chambersburg PA
CBHW080553030426
42337CB00024B/4856